Dedicated to my very own bird lovers

I KNOW THAT BIRD

Introducing young children to some
common birds of the back yard

Photos and text
by
Mauverneen Blevins

maureenblevins@yahoo.com
MauveOnTheMove.com

THIS BOOK BELONGS TO

Each morning I look out and see
a perky little Chickadee.
Little black cap upon his head
waiting for me -
he wants to be fed!

One fine day I looked outside
to see a Sparrow on the sill.
It sang to me a little song
for I was very still.

Robins are a sign of spring
when they come hopping by,

hunting worms for baby birds
and teaching them to fly.

Sometimes when I'm lucky,
the Orioles come along.
I feed them oranges and grape jelly
in exchange for their sweet song.

I always feel so special
when Buntings
come to call

They're small and shy and
bright bright blue
and don't stay long at all.

In summertime I love to watch the Hummingbirds whizz by.

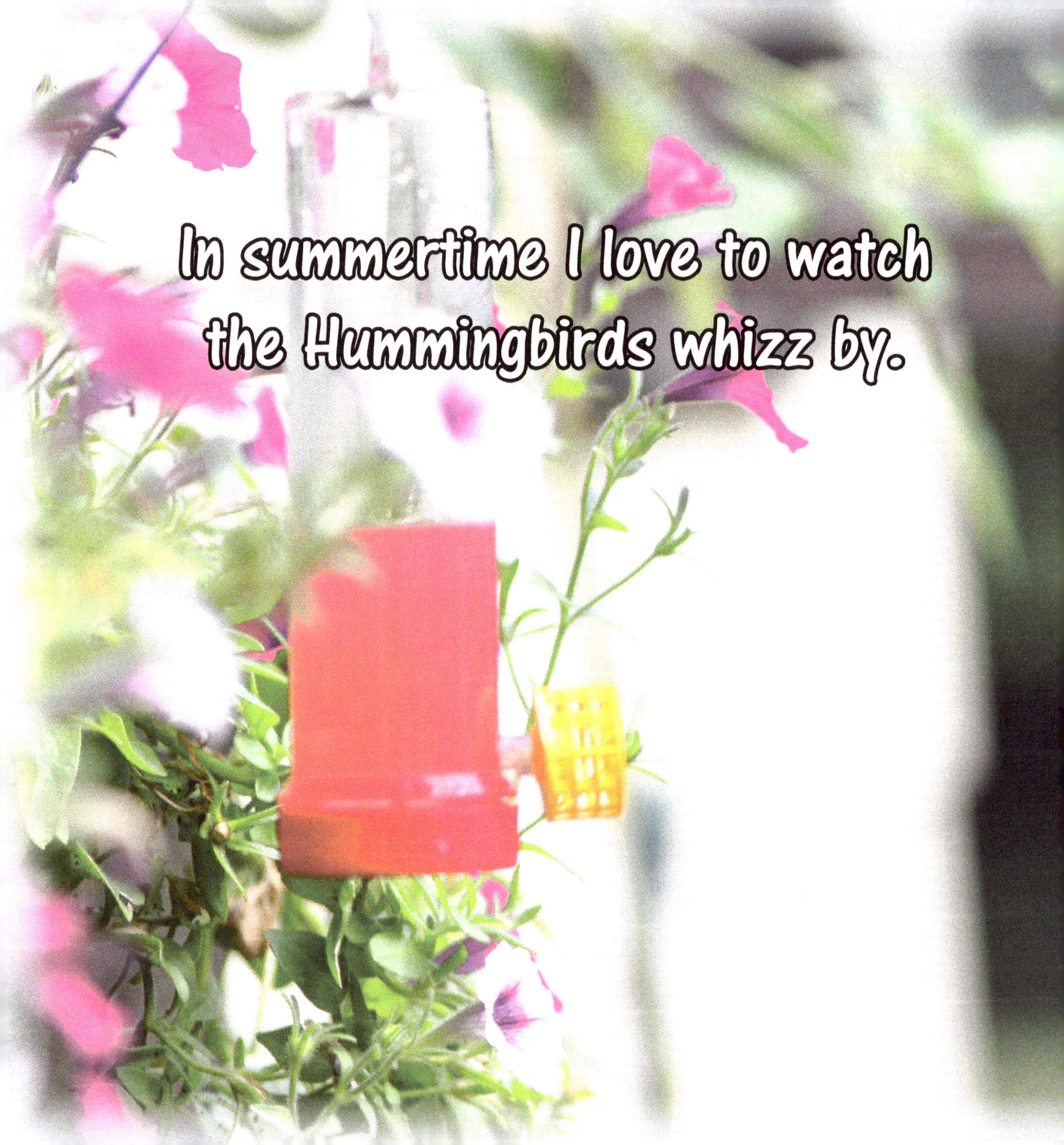

They stop to drink
then quick as a wink
away again they fly.

One cloudy, gloomy, boring day
some charming Finches
came to play.
Their sunny yellow feathers
sure did brighten up my day.

Little Wren, cute as can be
I wish you would come sit with me
I would promise you a treat
and be oh so still
while you sing so sweet.

I always hear before I see
a noisy Woodpecker close to me.
When I look up into the tree
he's knocking away,
as fast as can be.

I see Blue Jays all year 'round
In the air and on the ground.
They squawk and call as if to say
I want to eat and then let's play!

The Junco is a winter bird -

That's when it comes around.
It likes the cold and doesn't mind
when snow is on the ground.

I looked outside my window
one cold and snowy morn,

to find Mourning Doves
in the window box
trying to keep warm.

Bright red feathers
catch my eye
when Cardinals come flying by.

Winter, Spring, Summer, Fall,
They are my favorite of all.

It's oh so thrilling when I see
a Hawk up in the sky.
But when I see one
on the ground -
it's very large. Oh my!

I think it would be quite a hoot
to have an Owl in a tree
All evening asking who, hoo, hoo -
could he be asking me?

Chickadee
(Black-capped Chickadee)

Hummingbird
(Ruby Throated, male)

Oriole
(Baltimore Oriole, male)

Junco

Sparrow

Indigo Bunting
(male)

Carolina Wren

Finch
(American Goldfinch, male)

Woodpecker
(Red Bellied Woodpecker, male)

Robin
(American Robin)

Mourning Dove

Cardinal
(male and female)

Owl
(Great Horned Owl)

Blue Jay

Hawk
(Red-Tailed Hawk)

MY FAVORITE BIRD IS

_____